Where Is My Dad?

Written by

Ambry L. Ivy & Taylor Ivy

First edition

ISBN: 978-1-7362189-1-4

Illustration by Endi Astiko

For bulk orders and more information please visit www.taylorsmom.com

For my favorite girl in the whole wide world. You are my endless source of love and

inspiration. I love you.

-Ambry

For all of my family. I love you!

-Taylor

Taylor, at the school gate, sits and watches all her friends, as another school day ends.
Her Mommy comes to take young Taylor home like every day.
Today, though, Taylor has an urgent thing she wants to say:

"Mommy, I think it would be good,
if my Daddy came to pick me up — do you think he could?
"I'm sorry, Taylor, daddy can't pick you up today." Mommy replied

"You're always here to get me, but he *never* is, it's *not fair*.
It sometimes makes me wonder; do I have a dad at all?"

Mommy stops, kneels on one knee, and smiles at Taylor, but it's a strange, and funny smile – and Taylor wonders; "*What's about to change*?"

"Yes, you have a father Taylor dear, you really do. You can ask me anything you want about him too. You have a right to know and you should always ask, indeed. The truth is I just might not have the answers you need."

"I have so *many* questions, though, so many things I want to know.

What is he like? What *does* he like?
How come he doesn't live with us?
Does he drive a car? Or ride a bike?
Or take the train? Or the bus?
What does he like to drink? To eat?
His favorite program on TV?
Is he like you — kind, fun, and sweet?
But most importantly, does daddy love and care for me?"

"He never comes to see me in recitals for ballet,

he never comes to basketball; he never sees me play.

I want him to read me bedtime stories, but daddy's never there.

He doesn't come out to the park and swing me in the air.

He doesn't make my favorite food, or doesn't take me for ice cream.

He doesn't soothe me in bad moods, or when I'm so sad I could scream.

We never go out shopping, and we never go play ball.

I want to see my daddy, and I *never do* at all."

Mommy looks her in the eye, still bended on one knee,
"Taylor, dear, thank you *so much* for sharing this with me.
Your feelings are all valid — they're important, real, and true,
and bravely asking questions is the best thing you can do."

"Some dads are sleeping in heaven, and some dads live far away.
Some dads made poor choices and chose to stray,
while some dads were mean and had to go.
Some dads serve in the army, so,
there are many reasons some daddies aren't around.
Sadly, sometimes explanations why just can't be found.
If you look in the window of another home and see
a mom and dad, you *shouldn't* think, 'They're better than me.'"

"It's hard when questions don't have answers, it's really hard to bear,
when only he could answer them — I know that feels unfair.
Remember this —*you are loved* , and that will always be!
It's *not your fault* , you're still amazing, and not just only to me!
So many people care for you, your friends, and teachers too!
And me, I'm full of admiration, joy, and love for you."

"Taylor, this is how you show the world you're courageous and strong:
Forgive him , even though he can't say sorry he's done wrong."

Taylor looks around, and feels a warm breeze on her face.
The other kids all move about while Taylor stood in place.
A memory comes up — last week's recital for ballet,
she wished back then *he* could have seen her perfect-form passé.
And even so, she did it though! Her trophy's on the shelf!
She thought so much about him, she forgot about *herself* !

She blinks and thinks of basketball; the winning shot she scored!
Everyone was cheering; Taylor's name up on the board!
Her daddy wasn't there, no, but her *teammates* were so proud!
They showed her love, lifted her up, and called her name out loud!

She thinks of wishing he was there to read to her in bed,
but she can learn to read the stories to herself instead!

No, maybe she won't get to go for walks outside with dad,
but other kids invite her out; *she* makes *them* glad!

Daddy doesn't make her favorite food, but that's okay.

She helps Mom in the kitchen, and she'll cook for her someday.

"Now every time I think of dad and feel upset or blue,
I'll tell myself these things, which all are bold, and strong, and true:"

"I have a rhythm I march to, a rhythm that's all me,
and I'll never, ever lose touch with my creativity."

"I won't be counted as some lost, unknown number;
I will be an individual, imaginative, and a wonder!"

"I know I'm not to blame; I know it's not my fault at all.

I won't be made to feel because of this I'm weak, or small."

"When I look in the mirror, I am proud of what I see,
proud of my strength, proud of my bravery – I'm proud of *me*."

"I still have awesome friends and we still have lots of fun.
We laugh and play every day, I love and cherish every one."

"My life is full of love, even if my dad is not here to give it.

I know how to accept love, feel it, cherish it, and live it."

"I *won't* spend every day afraid of never knowing him,
and I *don't* have some great hole inside my soul I must fill in."

"This isn't my whole story, I have a whole long life to live, to find out how I'll grow, achieve, create and build, and give!"

"And best of all, my life is not some sad and tragic tale,
it's a story about *me*, and all the ways I can prevail."

"Mommy, can we kneel and say a special prayer tonight,
for every other child who finds they're fighting this same fight?"

"Dear God, for all the children thinking without fathers they can't cope,
please wipe away their tears, and wrap them up in joy and hope.
Happiness, fulfillment, peace and wellness still abound.
Their grace remains a part of them, and love is all around."

AFFIRMATIONS

ARE THINGS YOU THINK OR SAY ABOUT YOURSELF.

TAYLOR, MENTIONED SOME POSITIVE THINGS ABOUT HERSELF IN THE STORY.

YOU CAN PRACTICE WRITING POSITIVE AFFIRMATIONS ABOUT YOURSELF TOO!

AFTER WRITING YOUR AFFIRMATIONS, REPEAT THEM DAILY!

EXAMPLES:
I AM AN AMAZING PERSON
I AM A GREAT ARTIST
I AM BRAVE

I AM...

I CAN...

I AM GOOD AT...

NOW YOU TRY THIS ONE

Ambry is a Believer in Christ, a single-mother to a perfect little girl Taylor, author, blogger, educator, and world traveler. She is the youngest of seven children who were born and brought up in the northwest suburbs of Chicago, Illinois.

Ambry holds degrees of Bachelor of Arts in Criminal Justice and Master of Science in Cyber Security. Ambry currently works as an ESL teacher in Qingdao, China.

Because Ambry is generous and empathic, people are drawn to her motherly warmth and she becomes a safe haven where others can share their thoughts and ideas. She is also inquisitive, determined, and resourceful resulting in being walking proof of the dictum, "through Christ all things are possible". She strives to bring up Taylor in the fear and admonition of the Lord, all the while following her own dreams and encouraging others. Part of encouraging others is to ensure her daughter does not have a childhood she would need to recover from.

Ambry is an intercessor and enjoys praying for others. She has a special affection for single-mothers and seeks to encourage them to appreciate that, although, not an ideal situation, it is possible to make the best of single-motherhood with the help of the Lord. Her conviction is born out of the understanding there is no do-it-yourself manual or transcript on raising a child. She understands recovering from broken-heartedness is possible and firmly believes sharing her experiences will help others from committing common blunders.

Taylor is a powerful, brilliant, and confident four-year-old girl. She loves her family and friends. Taylor enjoys dancing, reading, playing with dolls, traveling, and helping others. When Taylor notices a problem, she takes the initiative to solve it. Her graceful, yet bold demeanor draws others to her charismatic energy, leaving her the "star" of any space she occupies. Taylor is a world traveler and had the unique experience of moving abroad to Qingdao, China with her mother at two years old. She has traveled to five countries, and over ten states in the United States. Taylor plans to continue to write books about her travels and world-schooling journey! If you ask Taylor what she wants to be when she grows up, she will be sure to say, "a wife, mother, pilot, and a doctor who deliver babies".

CPSIA information can be obtained
at www.ICGtesting.com
Printed in the USA
LVHW071546090721
692286LV00006B/246